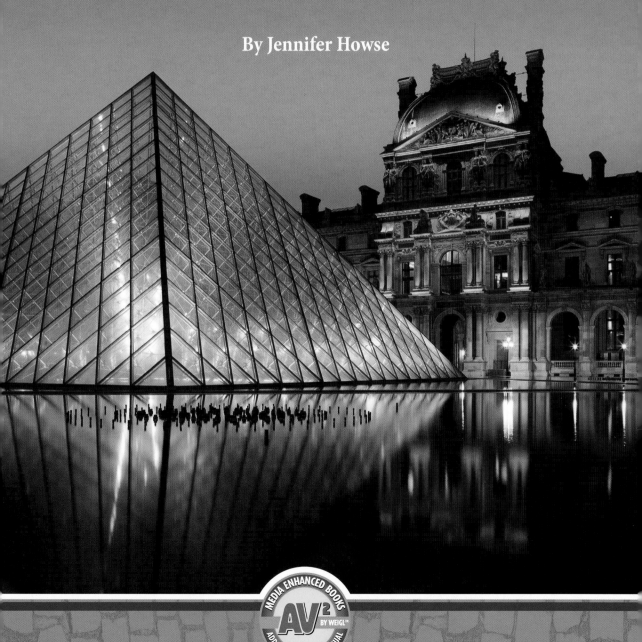

The Louvre

MUSEUMS OF THE WORLD

By Jennifer Howse

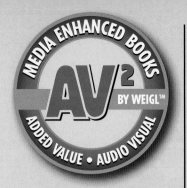

AV² provides enriched content that supplements and complements this book. Weigl's AV² books strive to create inspired learning and engage young minds in a total learning experience.

Your AV² Media Enhanced books come alive with...

Audio
Listen to sections of the book read aloud.

Key Words
Study vocabulary, and complete a matching word activity.

Video
Watch informative video clips.

Quizzes
Test your knowledge.

Embedded Weblinks
Gain additional information for research.

Slide Show
View images and captions, and prepare a presentation.

Try This!
Complete activities and hands-on experiments.

... and much, much more!

Go to **www.av2books.com**, and enter this book's unique code.

BOOK CODE

T986221

AV² by Weigl brings you media enhanced books that support active learning.

Published by AV² by Weigl
350 5th Avenue, 59th Floor
New York, NY 10118

Websites: www.av2books.com   www.weigl.com

Editor: Heather Kissock
Design: Dean Pickup

Every reasonable effort has been made to trace ownership and to obtain permission to reprint copyright material. The publishers would be pleased to have any errors or omissions brought to their attention so that they may be corrected in subsequent printings.

Weigl acknowledges Getty Images, Alamy, Art Resource Inc., Corbis, and Dreamstime as its primary image suppliers for this title.

Library of Congress Cataloging-in-Publication Data
Howse, Jennifer.
The Louvre / Jennifer Howse.
   pages cm. -- (Museums of the world)
Includes index.
ISBN 978-1-4896-1190-1 (hardcover : alk. paper) — ISBN 978-1-4896-1191-8 (softcover : alk. paper) —
ISBN 978-1-4896-1192-5 (single user ebk.) — ISBN 978-1-4896-1193-2 (multi user ebk.)
1. Musée du Louvre--Juvenile literature. 2. Art museums--France--Paris--Juvenile literature.
I. Title.
N2030.H66 2014
708.4'361--dc23
          2014006382

Printed in North Mankato, Minnesota, in the United States of America
1 2 3 4 5 6 7 8 9 0 18 17 16 15 14

032014
WEP150314

Contents

What Is the Louvre?

Deep in the heart of Paris, France, lies one of the world's largest and best-known museums. A visit to the Louvre, or *Musée du Louvre*, is a journey through hundreds of years of human activity and artistic effort. Works of art, symbols of history, and the big ideas of **humanity** are all on display in this former royal palace.

Museums are places that keep and protect the treasures of a culture. The **collections** in the Louvre represent some of the greatest discoveries and most beautiful expressions of human life. The artwork found in the Louvre's collections includes drawings, paintings, and sculptures. Many of these works tell the story of France's history. Others were collected by French explorers while on journeys to faraway places. These pieces help to tell the stories of ancient and exotic cultures and civilizations.

The Louvre covers a total area of approximately

652,300 square feet (60,600 square meters).

The Louvre has **460,000** works of art in its collection.

At any given moment, the Louvre has at least **35,000 items** on display.

It is estimated that it would take

9 months

just to glance at every piece of art in the Louvre.

The Louvre's pyramid was controversial when first completed, but is now recognized as a symbol of the museum.

History of the Louvre

The Louvre was originally constructed as a fortress on the west side of the city. It was meant to protect Paris from invading forces. As the city expanded past the fortress, however, the building could no longer serve as a defensive structure. It was eventually rebuilt as a royal palace and became the home of several French monarchs. The kings and queens who lived at the Louvre collected pieces of art from local and international artists, amassing a substantial collection. When the monarchy eventually abandoned the Louvre, the building began its transformation into an art gallery and museum.

Philippe Auguste ruled France from 1180 to 1223.

1190 A fortress called the Louvre is built by King Philippe Auguste.

1527–1560 The **medieval** building is torn down, and renovations take place to update the palace.

1200	1300	1400	1500

1364–1369 The Louvre becomes a royal residence.

1564–1572 A second palace, called the Tuileries, is built close to the Louvre. A long hallway called the *Petite Galerie* links the two palaces.

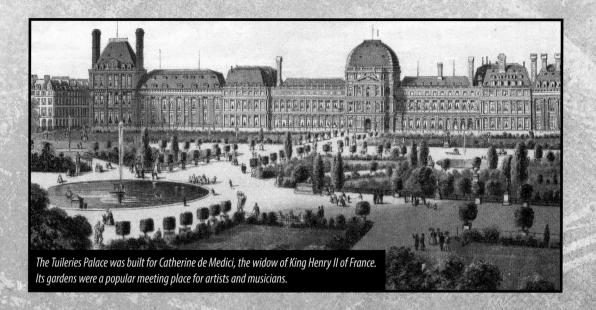

The Tuileries Palace was built for Catherine de Medici, the widow of King Henry II of France. Its gardens were a popular meeting place for artists and musicians.

1682 The king of France moves out of the Louvre to live in a new palace outside of Paris.

1871 Political activists set fire to the Tuileries, and it has to be torn down. The Louvre becomes the sole site of the museum.

1989 A glass pyramid is inaugurated in the Louvre's courtyard. It serves as the museum's main entrance.

1700   **1800**   **1900**   **2000**

1692 Three artist groups move into the buildings at the Louvre. Over time, they begin holding **salons** and art **exhibitions**.

1791 The French government proclaims that the Louvre and the Tuileries will become the home of art and science monuments for the country of France.

1981 The museum undergoes renovations to accommodate its growing collection and an increasing number of visitors.

The Founders

In 1793, the French government decided to open the *Museum Central des Arts* in the Louvre. Under the authority of the minister of the Interior, a committee was set up to organize the new institution. The committee comprised three painters, a designer, and an architect. This committee influenced the type of artwork collected and how it was displayed. Their vision can still be seen in the museum today.

Hubert Robert (1733–1808)

Robert was a painter who created **romantic** paintings of ancient ruins. He studied classic architecture in Italy, and applied what he learned there to his artwork. When he returned to Paris in 1765, his paintings of Italian landscapes received instant acclaim. This earned him admittance into the *Académie Royale de Peinture et de Sculpture*, an organization that assessed the quality of various works of art. As a Louvre governor, Hubert's main contribution to the museum was the design for the exhibit halls.

Robert was sometimes referred to as Robert des Ruines because so many of his paintings featured the ruins of buildings.

Jean-Honoré Fragonard (1732–1806)

Fragonard was a painter in the Rococo style, a style of art and design known for its whimsical approach to decoration. His interest in art was apparent early, and he began his career as an **apprentice** to two senior French artists. He later moved to Italy to study painting. When he returned to Paris, Fragonard was accepted into the *Académie Royale de Peinture et de Sculpture* and began accepting **commissions** from wealthy clients. His client base dwindled, however, as a result of the French Revolution, and he was asked to help with the creation of the Louvre. He eventually became one of the museum's first **curators**.

Fragonard produced more than 550 paintings over the course of his career.

François-André Vincent (1746–1816)

Vincent is considered one of the top neoclassical painters of his generation. Neoclassical art is known for its use of ancient Greek models and themes. Like many painters of the time, Vincent studied art in Rome. While there, he was awarded a prize called the *Prix de Rome* for his artwork. Upon his return to France, he taught art at the *Académie Royale de Peinture et de Sculpture*. It was on these qualifications that he was asked to become part of the Louvre's governing committee.

Vincent was only 22 years old when he received the Prix de Rome.

Augustin Pajou (1730–1809)

A sculptor and designer, Pajou's artwork and influence can still be seen in the Louvre. Another winner of the *Prix de Rome*, Pajou was elected to the *Académie Royale de Peinture et de Sculpture* in 1760. He was best known for his portraits and was the principal designer for the Versailles opera house. During the French Revolution, he was put in charge of protecting the country's monuments. In 1777, he was appointed keeper of the king's **antiquities**.

Pajou was raised in one of the poorer parts of Paris. His first art lessons came from his father, who was also a sculptor.

Charles de Wailly (1730–1798)

Wailly was an architect who studied classical Greek and Roman buildings. He was instrumental in bringing neoclassical architecture to France. Wailly designed several theaters in and around Paris, and later became a city planner. He was one of the few architects accepted into the *Académie Royale de Peinture et de Sculpture*. Wailly played an important role in designing the Louvre galleries. The Grande Gallery, which now houses sculptures of French kings, was his creation.

In 1752, Wailly left France to study architecture in Italy. He remained there for three years.

The Louvre Today

E ven though the Louvre is steeped in history, it has continued to develop with the times. In 1981, the Grand Louvre Project was launched. The project called for a large-scale renovation of the museum. Exhibit spaces were reorganized, and new features were introduced to handle the growing number of visitors. Today, a large, central lobby located under the glass pyramid provides visitors with access to tickets, galleries, and shops. Upon entering the museum, visitors can view even more artworks than in the past. The Grand Louvre Project brought about the opening of a new wing, as well as the creation of new display spaces in areas that were once outdoors.

The pyramid entrance takes visitors underground. The Cour Napoléon, the museum's central courtyard, had to be excavated to create space for the entrance.

Richelieu Wing

The Richelieu wing was home to government offices until 1981, when, as part of the Grand Louvre Project, it became part of the museum.

Sully Wing

The Sully wing is the oldest section of the Louvre. It forms a square around the Cour Corrée, an outdoor courtyard.

Denon Wing

The Denon wing runs along the right bank of the Seine River. The wing was named for Dominique Vivant, Baron Denon, the Louvre's first **director**.

Tuileries Gardens

The Tuileries Gardens lie to the west of the Louvre. The gardens are home to a small decorative lake, 2,860 trees, and a variety of flowers.

Pyramid Entrance

The glass and metal pyramid was designed by renowned architect I. M. Pei. It is accompanied by three smaller pyramids, as well as reflecting pools and fountains.

Touring the Louvre

Each of the Louvre's wings is made up of four floors. These floors feature galleries that showcase works from the Louvre's various curatorial departments. Most of the galleries have a theme, which can range from the type of **artifacts** displayed to the era of their creation.

Sully Wing Visitors to the first floor of the Sully wing have the opportunity to walk around the remains of the medieval castle that once stood on the site. The second and third floors feature antiquities from Greece and Egypt. French paintings from the 18th and 19th centuries are housed on the fourth floor.

The Louvre's collection of Egyptian antiquities is spread over 30 rooms.

At one time, the Gallery of Apollo connected the Louvre to the Tuileries Palace. Today, it houses a collection that includes paintings, sculptures, and the crown jewels of France.

Denon Wing The first and second floors of the Denon wing feature European sculptures from the 11th to 19th centuries, although significant space on the first floor is devoted to Greek, Etruscan, and Roman antiquities. Italian art is the focus of the third floor. The fourth floor is not open to the public.

Richelieu Wing French sculptures cover much of the first two floors of the Richelieu wing. The third floor galleries feature artifacts from the Middle Ages, **Renaissance**, and **Restoration**. The fourth floor galleries display paintings from German, Flemish, and Dutch artists.

The Rubens Room, on the second floor of the Richelieu wing, features 24 paintings by Flemish artist Peter Paul Rubens.

Napoleon III Apartments The second floor of the Richelieu wing is also home to Napoleon III's apartments. Napoleon III was the French emperor from 1852 to 1870. Gold-gilded ceilings and glittering chandeliers decorate each room.

A tour through Napoleon's apartments allows visitors to experience the opulent lifestyle of French royalty in the 19th century.

The Louvre's pyramid is made up of almost **800 panes of glass.**

Napoleon's apartments feature a chandelier that measures 9 feet (2.7 m) across.

More than **2,000** people work at the Louvre.

The Louvre plays host to about **8 million** visitors each year.

67% of the Louvre's annual visitors are from other countries.

In the winter, the Louvre offers free admission on the first Sunday of every month.

During World War II, most of the Louvre's collections were removed from the building for protection.

The Sully wing has a sphinx that is more than

4,000

years old.

The Louvre has at least

4,000 paintings

by French artists alone.

The *Mona Lisa* is covered with a sheet of bulletproof glass.

The Louvre's collection features works from the

6th century BC to the 19th century AD.

The 2014 restoration of the Winged Victory of Samothrace cost more than

$5 million.

Treasures of the Louvre

Museums collect works of art for many different reasons. If an artist is known to represent a style or period of time, his or her work may be prized. Other works may be collected because of what they symbolize. A painting, for example, may tell the story of an important historical event. Many of the world's best-known and most treasured works of art are found in the Louvre's galleries. Some of these are the works of master artists. Others represent a specific time and place.

All museums, including the Louvre, arrange exhibits by theme. This helps people understand the context of the works.

Winged Victory of Samothrace Created between 220 and 185 BC, this sculpture is considered a masterpiece of **Hellenistic** art. The sculpture shows Nike, the goddess of victory, standing on the prow of a ship. She is facing into the wind, causing her clothing to billow around her. The piece is known for its theatricality and strong sense of movement.

Winged Victory was found on the Greek island of Samothrace in the mid-1800s.

Mona Lisa Painted between 1503 and 1506 by Italian artist Leonardo da Vinci, the *Mona Lisa* is perhaps the most visited artwork in the Louvre. People have spent centuries trying to interpret the reason for the subject's slight smile.

The Mona Lisa is believed to portray the wife of an Italian merchant.

Bed from Château d'Effiat This bed is a rare piece of intact 17th-century bedroom furnishing. Made from the wood of a walnut tree, the four-poster canopy bed is itself quite simple. It is its velvet and silk **tapestry** that suggests luxury and wealth.

The canopy bed resided in the Château d'Effiat until 1856. It is now on loan to the Louvre.

Egyptian Book of the Dead Exhibited in the Sully wing are fragments from the Egyptian Book of the Dead. Painted on papyrus, these rolls of hieroglyphics were placed in tombs. They were meant to protect the deceased. The fragments on display at the Louvre are believed to protect against hunger.

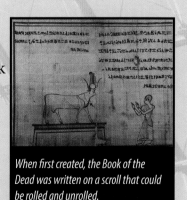

When first created, the Book of the Dead was written on a scroll that could be rolled and unrolled.

Collection Conservation

One of the most important roles of a museum is to **conserve** its collection. All museum workers share the responsibility of ensuring the artworks are saved for people in the future to enjoy. Conservators, however, are the people directly involved with maintaining the condition of each piece of art or artifact. Conservators use a variety of techniques to assess the condition of each piece. They then take steps to protect it and prevent any further damage or deterioration.

Photography One of the best ways to understand if a piece of art is damaged is to examine it very closely. Photographing a painting at an oblique angle creates a **raking light**. This raking light will reveal flaws, cracks, or flakes in the paint that may need repair.

Conservators use a variety of techniques to assess the condition of works in their collections.

Lighting Shining light on artwork is a necessary part of displaying it. However, light can damage and fade many of the materials used to create art. Conservators work closely with curators to determine the type and amount of light that should be shone on a piece of art. Sometimes, timers are used to control the amount of light. An object may also be put into storage from time to time to give it a rest from the light.

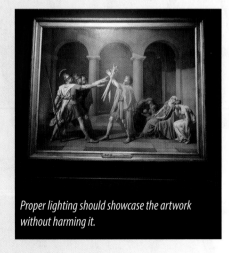

Proper lighting should showcase the artwork without harming it.

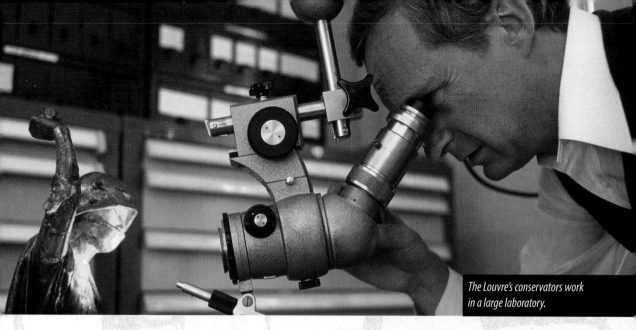

The Louvre's conservators work in a large laboratory.

Climate Control Artifacts made from wood are sensitive to **humidity** levels. Low humidity makes the wood dry and brittle. High humidity causes the wood to absorb the moisture and swell. Conservators often place items that are vulnerable to humidity in glass display cases with a humidifier. The humidifier helps monitor and control the amount of moisture reaching the artifact.

Display cases allow conservators to better control the environment around an artifact.

Cleaning Over time, a piece of art can become dirty. Conservators have to know the best way to clean the artwork so that its true colors are restored and it is not damaged in the process. Artwork is often cleaned using brushes and vacuums. Sometimes, an **aqueous** solution is applied to the art to provide a deeper cleaning.

Conservators often use magnifying lenses when cleaning to ensure that nothing is removed from the painting that should not be.

The Louvre in the World

Besides preserving and displaying artwork and artifacts, the Louvre also serves as a place of learning. It runs several programs that allow people to learn more about art and culture. These programs are sometimes held within the museum itself. The museum also has **outreach** programs that allow it to connect with people throughout the world.

School Programs The Louvre is committed to giving schoolchildren a chance to interact with its collection. In 2009, it announced plans to develop its Art Suitcase Program. This program will provide teachers with kits that can be used on museum visits or in the classroom. The kits will include art samples, games, and videos. The Louvre also plans to place study stations throughout the museum. These stations will contain information about items found in the collection.

The Louvre has a team of official guides available to take school groups on tours through the galleries.

Traveling Exhibits Not everyone can go to France to visit the Louvre. To give people in other parts of the world the opportunity to view pieces from its collection, the Louvre sometimes loans artworks to other museums. These works are often loaned as part of a themed collection. Visitors can view a sampling of art or artifacts in a specific context and learn more about their place in history.

The Louvre loans its works to museums all over the world. In 2005, it sent an exhibit of French art to China.

Lectures The Louvre's curators are experts in their fields. They often share their knowledge by giving talks on the Louvre's collections and the work they do. Often, the public can attend a talk at the Louvre. Curators also post videos online that people can access from anywhere in the world. The Louvre's curators are sometimes invited to speak internationally, providing people in other countries with the opportunity to learn more about the museum.

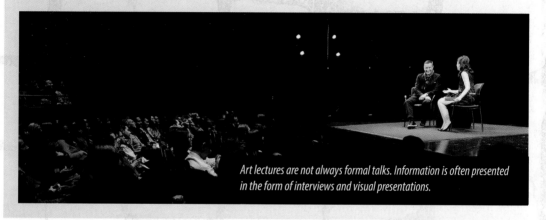

Art lectures are not always formal talks. Information is often presented in the form of interviews and visual presentations.

Satellite Museums In 2012, the Louvre opened a **satellite branch** in the French city of Lens. The goal of the satellite branch is to expand the reach of the Louvre while also helping the city's economy. The museum at Lens exhibits works from the Paris Louvre's collections and hosts temporary exhibits of its own. To extend the Louvre's reach further, it was announced in 2007 that the Louvre will open its first international branch in Abu Dhabi, a city in the United Arab Emirates. This museum will feature artwork from the Paris Louvre, as well as several other French museums.

The Louvre Lens' exhibit spaces are encased in a framework of aluminum, steel, and glass, giving the building an open atmosphere.

Looking to the Future

The Louvre is an active, progressive institution that continues to evolve with the times. Its satellite branches are just one way that the museum is working to find new audiences and extend its reach. Inside the Louvre itself, curators are always looking for new ways to present the museum's collections. New galleries were recently created to host the museum's Islamic arts collection, and more space is being readied to house the expanding collection of Greek, Roman, and Etruscan works. In the long term, the museum is working to create a center for heritage preservation, research, and restoration. The center will allow the Louvre to maintain its collections so that future generations can experience and discover the cultural treasures held within the Louvre.

The Louvre's new Islamic Arts gallery opened in 2012, housing artifacts that cover at least 1,300 years of history.

The Louvre Abu Dhabi was designed by prize-winning architect Jean Nouvel. Two-thirds of the museum is covered by a dome that is meant to represent palm leaves.

Activity

O ne tool that curators use to share their knowledge of a piece of art is a text panel. A text panel is a placed at the entrance of an exhibit or beside an art display. On the panel is information about the art on display. Curators can include information on the artwork such as the name of the artist, when the artwork was created, or what style the artist used. The purpose of a text panel is to inform visitors to the museum about the artwork they are seeing and what the curator thinks is important about the display.

Imagine that you are one of the Louvre's curators. Go to the Louvre's website, and find an artwork or artifact that interests you. Study the artwork closely, and then write a text panel of no more than 50 words for that piece of art. Imagine that this panel will be placed beside the work of art in the Louvre to help visitors understand more about the artwork. What information would you like to share that would help someone else see the artwork in a new way?

Use the questions below to help you create your text panel.

1. What is the title?

2. Who is the artist?

3. Where did the piece come from?

4. What type of art or object is it?

5. What is it made of?

6. What is the size?

7. Who may have owned it or used it?

8. Why is it important?

Louvre Quiz

1 Where is the Louvre located?

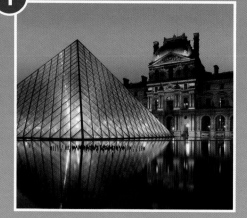

2 What type of building was the Louvre when it was first built in the 12th century?

3 Name the Louvre's three main wings.

4 Who painted the *Mona Lisa*?

5 Where was the Louvre's first satellite branch established?

ANSWERS:

1. Paris, France **2.** A fortress **3.** Sully, Richelieu, and Denon **4.** Leonardo da Vinci **5.** Lens, France

Key Words

antiquities: objects from ancient times

apprentice: a person who works with another to learn a trade

aqueous: of, like, or containing water

artifacts: objects that were made by people in the past

collections: works of art or other items collected for exhibit and study in a museum, and kept as part of its holdings

commissions: the hiring and payment for the creation of art

conserve: to protect an object from deterioration

curators: people who manage, study, and care for a museum collection

director: the person in charge of an institution or organization

exhibitions: displays of objects or artwork within a theme

Hellenistic: relating to Greek culture

humanity: human beings collectively

humidity: moisture in the air

medieval: a period between 500 AD and 1500 AD, also called the Middle Ages

outreach: the process of bringing information or services to people

raking light: a bright light used to reveal texture and detail

Renaissance: a period between 1500 AD and 1800 AD

Restoration: a period that occurred in France between 1814 and 1830

romantic: art that emphasizes feeling and content over form and order

salons: receptions

satellite branch: a facility physically separated but dependent on another facility

tapestry: a heavy cloth woven with colorful designs

Index

Log on to www.av2books.com

AV² by Weigl brings you media enhanced books that support active learning. Go to www.av2books.com, and enter the special code found on page 2 of this book. You will gain access to enriched and enhanced content that supplements and complements this book. Content includes video, audio, weblinks, quizzes, a slide show, and activities.

AV² Online Navigation

Book Pages
AV² pages directly correspond to pages in the book.

Key Words
Study vocabulary, and complete a matching word activity.

Quizzes
Test your knowledge.

Slide Show
View images and captions, and prepare a presentation.

Audio
Listen to sections the book read alo

Video
Watch informative video clips.

Embedded Weblink
Gain additional information for research.

Try This!
Complete activities and hands-on experiments.

AV² was built to bridge the gap between print and digital. We encourage you to tell us what you like and what you want to see in the future.

Sign up to be an AV² Ambassador at www.av2books.com/ambassador.